FUGITIVE HORIZONS

ESSENTIAL POETS SERIES 205

Canada Council **Conseil des Arts**
for the Arts **du Canada**

ONTARIO ARTS COUNCIL
CONSEIL DES ARTS DE L'ONTARIO
50 YEARS OF ONTARIO GOVERNMENT SUPPORT OF THE ARTS
50 ANS DE SOUTIEN DU GOUVERNEMENT DE L'ONTARIO AUX ARTS

Guernica Editions Inc. acknowledges the support of
the Canada Council for the Arts and the Ontario Arts Council.
The Ontario Arts Council is an agency of the Government of Ontario.
We acknowledge the financial support of the Government of Canada through the National Translation
Program for Book Publishing for our translation activities.
We acknowledge the financial support of the Government of Canada through the Canada Book Fund
(CBF) for our publishing activities.

HENRY BEISSEL

FUGITIVE HORIZONS

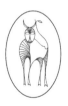

GUERNICA
TORONTO – BUFFALO – LANCASTER (U.K.)
2013

Michael Mirolla, editor
Guernica Editions Inc.
P.O. Box 76080, Abbey Market, Oakville, (ON), Canada L6M 3H5
2250 Military Road, Tonawanda, N.Y. 14150-6000 U.S.A.

Distributors:
University of Toronto Press Distribution,
5201 Dufferin Street, Toronto (ON), Canada M3H 5T8
Gazelle Book Services, White Cross Mills, High Town, Lancaster LA1 4XS U.K.

First edition.
Printed in Canada.
Legal Deposit – Third Quarter
Library of Congress Catalog Card Number: 2013933970
Library and Archives Canada Cataloguing in Publication
Beissel, Henry, 1929-
Fugitive horizons / Henry Beissel.
(Essential poets series ; 205)
Poems.
Also issued in electronic format.
ISBN 978-1-55071-732-7
I. Title. II. Series: Essential poets series ; 205
PS8503.E39F84 2013   C811'.54   C2013-901445-4

CONTENTS

I HORIZONS

II FUGITIVE

To John Smith

in celebration of a friendship:
a sixty-year dialogue
and fellowship of minds
that continue...

Once the first drop fell – it was a kind of splat
on a lens previously crystal-clear and focused on
infinity – everything that has since become the case
acquired the prestige of the inevitable.

John Smith, *Fireflies in the Magnolia Grove*

I

HORIZONS

...for the mind to walk, barefoot, into its own undoing...

A Pied Carpet for the Mind

Stretch the strands grasses string to the clouds
and loop the plotlines of your facts and fictions round them,
then extend the gothic surge of trees far into the sky
so that ocean waves can fishtail their crests between them,

next, hang your thoughts higher than mountain peaks
and let their loose ends trail on the ground to grow roots,
attach the flicker of candle-flames to the phases of the moon,
pick your shadow off the floor and pin it to a distant star,

now tie the fugitive horizons into a knot that holds earth
to heaven, and using the formula flowers apply to sunlight
weave animal tracks across the seasons' curved space,
finally compact the fabric with the reed poets employ,

and there you have it – a pied carpet for the mind to walk,
barefoot, into its destined undoing and thus come into its own.

To Salute the Sky

There are two putative ways which promise to get you
there. One, horizontally, on the solar pyre that burns
everything back to the beginning, is the popular western
route across the prairies; the other, the eastern route,
winds vertically up from the coast and across mountain
ranges raising fists full of fossils to salute the sky.

There's a third path that goes straight down, but they say
it's the same as the one up, except it's more dangerous,
more precipitous. The fourth dimension is really just a map
so you can find your way into the fifth dimension which is
virtually impossible to enter and in the cardinal mode leads
to a geometry of the infinite that's three times larger than it is.

I'm partial to mountain passes; they call for mind games
that prepare you for what you'll find when you get there.

We're Secrets

We're secrets to ourselves and the trillions
of microbes that walk us daily through all
the many formulas of living without giving
anything away. We're noisy cooperatives
of microbes that took a thousand million years
to learn to be different, each at its special post
following and guarding life's coded instructions.

We're messages from one microbe to another
multiplied a hundred trillion times, written
in a language of fragile fictions that define
the syntax of our bodies and our minds
in every cell. Sometimes they make mistakes
because microbes don't know they know
the secret for which we have no words.

Cosmic Auditorium

It's just possible that all is music and dance,
that all matter and force is composed of and by
strings, that the whole cosmic performance
from the opening fortissimo to the final tutti
is orchestrated by strings so tiny we'll never
be able to ascertain whether or not they exist.

Make no mistake: the mind dances to the tune
of invisible orchestras, each trillions of strings,
playing up worlds of facts, fictions, and fancies
in the auditorium of every raindrop, every galaxy,
every moment of silence the mind dances
circles round itself to define the night's horizons.

We hulahoop our way through the universe, each
the centre of what might or might not be true.

Something to Talk About

I've been telling you for over four hundred years
the stars don't turn around you, they turn you around,
and still you're giving every day the lie, calling dawn
sunrise and nightfall sunset. I know you can't see
straight, but I thought it was because light is bent,
not because you're at your wits' end. You want more

proof? Thank your lucky stars you don't feel the headwind
as you're spun around this topsy-turvy stellar carrousel.
At a galactic speed of well over half a million miles per hour
it'd blow you away. Then you'd have something to talk about.

Enjoy a walk in the forest instead. Smell the cedars, listen
to the waxwings and warblers, watch the deer, touch the moss.
You're moving in at least four different directions at once:
one of them will take you right back to where you started.

On Night's Edge

Countless universes have come to nothing. A thousand
septillionths of a second into what might have become
another time a zillion particles collided with a zillion
anti-particles and vanished before they had ever been.

You stand by night's edge and listen to the wind
bring in the stars on a black tide. Darkness soon comes
in huge waves across light years and sweeps you up
in its surf to ride the shoreline of thought into a spinning
sparkling funnel from which you never re-emerge.

Were you or did you become a function of that interstellar wave?
How many histories has your species been written into?
Were they all life-and-death gambles in a game of chance?

Words and numbers fail you, but you determine
to name and measure your failures and record them as truths.

In the Green Labyrinth

Ah yes, truth – now there's a thought to inspire passion
in the best and the worst, as only a woman of beauty can.
We adore her, desire her, pursue her frantic to possess her,
we want the truth, the whole truth and nothing but the truth

so badly we strip her and drag her naked through the streets,
we buy and sell her favours, try to force her to reveal all, and
when she hides we applaud those who discover and expose her.
Are we cursed forever to abuse and batter what we love?

It's not love that's blind, but lust. That's why we fail
to understand that truth is secretive by nature. Like all things
beautiful, she is shy, elusive, mysterious, and hides her virtues,
withdraws when you come too close to her, in confusion.

If we could learn to accept what disdains us, learn what it is to love,
we might find what we seek in the green labyrinth that confines us.

The Honest Truth

You want to know the honest truth (not the one
we circulate to keep up appearances)? *We create
each other.* So, now you know, now you don't.
Know that those four words repudiate the mind/
body split and prove the mortality of your immortal
soul. Your flesh is the honest truth of your spirit.

Grief and loss can break the unbreakable heart:
cortisol will rampage through your body in search
of lymphocytes to kill, leaving you defenceless to
pathogens. Unhappy lovers do die from a broken
heart for the body understands the mind's messages.

What about happy lovers? Do they live forever?
Or does love obey the second law of thermodynamics?

Life depends on what you don't know that you know –
the secrets of enzymes and hormones about proteins,
and the whims of microbes whose mobile home we are.

Put Your Ear to It

No one and nothing prepared us for infinity. You can't see it, you can't
hear it, but if you didn't believe in it you couldn't draw a single line,
for a point has no length and it takes any number of points to get from A
to B, and infinitely more to reach Z. Mathematicians had to invent zero

first, but you can't see or hear naught either. So they drew a circle round
a hole. That didn't amount to much. So they drew two circles round two
holes, connected them, and bingo they got infinity ∞ = two holes. Except
that there must be an infinity of infinities. Story-tellers call those zeros
gods – they can't be seen or heard either, but you can smell the incense.

Listen to Bach's or Beethoven's fugues and you'll come across moments
of infinity though they were deaf and blind. A shepherd's flute in the mountains
can fly you there too. Or a master's cello. It took three billion years to prepare

us for that music. A paradox is the key in which infinity writes its tunes;
it doesn't open the door to its mysteries but you can put your ear to it.

The Music of the Spheres

If you think mathematics is the soul of music
you have another thing coming – namely photons.
Those critters elude calculation: they have no substance
and when they bump into each other they split in two
and each of them does exactly what the other does
though they're instantly thousands of miles apart.

That's how you can know what happens elsewhere
and elsewhen, because it happens also here and now.
Put that in your pipe dreams and see if it'll light up
your sleep. To imagine you imagine the universe to be
ruled by the optics of your brain. You don't get it

because you're not listening: the music of the spheres
is heard inside out. So much for your theorems and equations.

May I Have this Tango?

If every particle in the universe is a single,
identical, one-dimensional, Planck-length string,
it takes a hundred sextillion (10^{17}) of them to compose
the nucleus of a single atom. The difference
between the moon, a mouse, and the Sistine Chapel,
between a mirror, a comet, and the smell of a rose,
between my heart and the hand writing these lines,
is all and only in the way the strings vibrate,
the dicey way the vibrations dance into melody
across eleven different indifferent dimensions.

Each of us could be the echo of a tune played
in one of the seven dimensions we cannot know.

May I have this tango, Miss Universe, so that
I can dance you into the seventh heaven of love?
There's no one else out there in interstellar space
who can make you such an offer and follow through.

A Paradox for Galileo

How many blades of grass make up a mountain meadow,
a prairie landscape, or a whole summer's free-range pasture?
Every one of them hardens its tip in the bluehot wind
and takes a stab at the sky before raising its seeds to the stars
waiting for the regular rainwash to keep the light dustfree.

Ideas ripen thus from green saplings to golden harvest,
the same multitude, the same patient sharpening of edges,
the same thrust beyond words and meaning – the same final
judgment under the second law of thermodynamics:
everything is sentenced to return forever diminished.

Even if the universe has no boundaries, there must be
more natural than square numbers because the gaps
between the latter grow by leaps and bounds. Yet all
natural numbers can be squared. A paradox for Galileo.

Others Are Writing this Poem

Not even a blind man should be surprised to find
planets circling other suns elsewhere. Sight
was never a necessary condition for existence.
The four forces that move the universe play

by the rules of chance. No birth is without blood
or placenta. Where stars are born in the centripetal
crunch of particles planetesimals rush into orbit.

You know the forest not from counting trees
or measuring them, but from understanding
process in the presence of light and water.

From the leftovers of starbirths planets assemble
destinies enough to defy your comprehension:
on one of them someone else is writing this poem.

Celebrate the Flaw

In the beginning there was nothing and nothing
exploded to create an inferno finely balanced
to annihilate itself faster than the speed of light
so that no one would ever know it happened.
In that balance hung the fate of the universe.

It was meant to be a blip – someone's whim in one
of the seven other dimensions, and it would've come
to nothing but for the tiniest flaw in the symmetry
of mutual destruction between particle and antiparticle:
one quark survived for every billion extinctions.

Was the flaw in the formula? Was a law infringed?
Is every universe the fruit of error or transgression?

I hold you to your promise to dine with me tonight
to celebrate the flaw to which we owe this flawed world.

He Walks Across the Night

Evening stretches its dark tentacles to coil around every object in sight,
sucking the light off the roofs of buildings and down from the crowns
of trees, and slowly strangles every last beam twisting on the ground.

That's how cities sprawl, pulling the green cover off fields and choking
the living daylights out of the soil. Of gardens, only the gates are left,
shut against a horizon where black flowers flee the saw-toothed skyline.

Is it the dark that devours the light and eats the heart of every star
till at the end of time all that remains is their ashes scattered across
a vast emptiness? Or will the billions of suns torch all the world's
shadows and we go home to another universe in a blaze of light?

A midsummer night comes to mind when he made love under the stars
to her with the luminous body. What if he had learnt to love her truly?

He walks wistful across the night along the Milky Way and marvels
that the spinning galaxies of roaring infernos we call stars are so still.

A Picnic for the Mind

What you have to understand is that your ignorance
is a function of your knowledge. Try as you will
to understand why or even whether the world is
what it appears to be, and all you will discover
is your ignorance which surfaces as insight.

Wisdom unteaches and unlearns everything.
A sage adds spice to the stew of misconceptions,
letting us savour the irreconcilable ingredients
in experience. There's no recipe to prepare
the mind's meals: you use your imagination.

Let's have our picnic with the birds and the lilies
in the valley at the foot of the holy mountain of silence,
lying in the grass that is as the flesh,
drinking day and night away as we embrace
                                        the dark.

Getting Darker Still

It's difficult to come to terms with a universe
which absolutely disdains to take you seriously,
especially when your sole *raison d'être* is to talk.

We've spun words into any number of imaginable worlds,
but none of them seem to match the one we inhabit.
We can't even agree that god is a dog spelled backwards.

There was a time before time could be measured
when the universe was nothing but sky – huge, hot,
reddish glowing, a balloon blowing itself up and out
of all proportion with nothing of purpose or prospect.

That's why the nights are dark and getting darker still:
that bubble is still there, light millennia across now,
cooling down to blackness. The little coloured flags
we've stuck all over the map won't deceive the stars.

Tracings in Silver Dust

When you seek a truth at the heart of things
you become the victim of your own paradigm.
Peel away the skin of an onion and all you get
is layer after layer of onion – and tears in your eyes.

Plato's parable is true only if none of the prisoners
in the cave breaks the chains. Philosophers too see
only the shadow of things and abstract from them,
at best, the tricky convoluted mechanics of their mind.

Ah, but how colourful these shadows! How they sing
and dance through the forests of our lives! Things are
what they appear to be in the fullness of our senses –
charged with joy and sorrow: both bring tears to our eyes.

The delicate soft designs on the wings of moths light up
the night's eyes though they are but tracings in silver dust.

This Dawn Happens

This dawn happens like every other dawn once only
in a universe. The way the sun pops in slow motion
from the hidden furnace of night dripping molten gold,
passes through thin layers of clouds and re-emerges

radiant as Apollo, is unique. All the fractions and refractions,
all their curved angles and edges, motions and directions,
are irreversible – like the patterns half the world's flowers
make of light, turning their petals away from the wind,
and the tales half the world's creatures live scurrying
into burrows or mimicry and camouflage – all is irrevocable.

This universe cannot replay this dawn or recreate its patterns,
even if dark matter should reverse its course. Invisible
gravitons can only pull us back into another singularity.
This dawn's complexity remains uniquely and forever mine.

Quantum Dualities

One morning he looked into the mirror
and found himself face to face with someone other
than himself who was nevertheless herself.

Advanced mathematics confirmed the elastic fabric
of the universe could, if stretched to infinity, tear
and create quantum psychology in the crack.

Was the cosmos tearing itself apart over
the numbers game he was playing so skilfully
that it left his double to fend for herself?

The other stalked him into high noon, then fled
past the meridian and vanished over the horizon
of darkness where they were reunited. In his sleep

she talked to a stranger bearing her name, and he
knew him to be who she would be in the morning.

At the Speed of Light

The faster you move the longer you live: the clock
slows down as you speed up and, according to Einstein,
at the speed of light it stops. I know around 300,000 km/sec
you yourself become light. Are you dead then or immortal?

When time stands still space collapses. Is light then forever
everywhere? Or nowhere? Without spacetime there can be
no speed either. So what are we measuring? How vast is vast
when predicated on a tiny redshift in an instantaneous cosmos?

Of course Einstein got a lot of things wrong, or only half-right,
like the idea that god doesn't play dice with the universe, or
the time he let a rabbi's rabid son talk him into signing a letter
asking the President to give his blessing to use the atomic bomb.

So he played the violin a lot and hazarded equations. After all,
the universe is a game of hazard, and no one else is playing it.

The Golden Apple

The logic of religion starts with the premise
that apple trees bear fruit so that we can enjoy
Apfelstrudel, and cows oblige with heavy cream
to whip into gustatory orgasm – isn't God divine?!

The same benevolence may not be so evident
in metaphor: the apple the snake talked Eve into
seduced Adam's generations into thinking they were
exiles from God's orchard – makes sense, doesn't it?!

Paris awarded the golden apple to Aphrodite
on the premise that the universe means to be
beautiful. Thinking proceeds from the same judgment.

Plato awarded the golden apple to Socrates
on the premise that the universe means to be true.
If beauty is the differential can we calculate truth?

The windfall apple that landed on Newton's mind
struck a familiar chord – a thud such as thinking makes
when it falls for the charms of norms and numbers.

Hauling Genes

If you're wondering why life is such a burden
remember the genome: a tome the size
of eight hundred Bibles, and you carry
a hundred trillion copies of it around with you
everywhere, all the time. And most of it is junk.

It's a book of recipes: how to prepare protein
for every occasion. But it's full of mistakes, some
made copying – a word, a letter left out here, added
there, instructions repeated over and over, plus reams
of gibberish, obsolete ingredients which didn't survive
the proof in the eating or being eaten. Cold pudding
when one wrong letter can cost you your life.

We're mules hauling a load of manure on a mountain trail
from generation to generation to deliver a handful of seeds.

Answers and Questions

Answers and questions do not relate to each other
as keys and locks do. Rather they form hinges
on which a door swings between now and then,
much as you and I do, on the threshold of death.

Every answer is composed of countless questions
waiting to break free from the illusion of finality.
Salmon labour upriver to spawn, burst into a million
replicas of themselves and return to the sea. Massive
stars in their fiery death throes seed dark interstellar fields.

The alphabet is no answer to the question of existence.
Borges calculated that all the possible combinations
of twenty-six letters would fill books only a library
the size of the universe could house. The mind is
a question to which this universe is one of many answers.

The Mathematics of Love

When we have counted all the unruly atoms in the sea and all
the stars in the unfathomed sky, when we have numbered the myriad
stairs in the double helix of life and the incalculable permutations
of energy and matter in a universe where everything possible comes
to pass, when we have mapped every nook and cranny in the molecule,
the genome, and the Milky Way, measured the weight of gravity and
light, the distance between one elusive electron and another, computed
the time between the birth of the first particle and the first living cell,
between the first quiver of brainpower in annelid worms and its last
spasm in the nuclear bomb – when we have accomplished all that,
shall we be gods, as the serpent in the tree of knowledge promised?

That evening, as the shadows of trillions of trees stretched over fugitive
horizons, he leaned over her to watch the stars dance in her eyes
by the mathematics of love that holds the mystery in their embrace.

The Certainty of Silence

One thing is certain: there can be no certainty.
Make me a map of a bat's flight-path for tonight.
Or paint me the shape and position of a single cloud
in tomorrow morning's sky. Where is the raindrop
I watched trickle down a window pane yesterday?

If God existed he'd be blind. Because he couldn't be sure
about anything, for he couldn't know both the position and
the speed of any particle any place any time. Like you and me,
he'd be in the dark about a universe where any god would need
to be light – and cease to be. *Contradictio in rerum natura.*

When we are gone and lichen have repossessed the stones
we cut into cities, when wind and rain have levelled even
the temples we built for gods we cloned from ourselves,
the silence we leave behind will tell all we ever knew.

Silence

Let there be silence. Stop the forward engines,
shut off all machines and stay your tongue –
I want to listen to the sun's choir in the open air
auditorium of the forest that makes the sap dance
to its tune under the bark of every tree. I want to hear
what the wind is telling the flowers as it stalks
the fields with a message from the faraway sea.

Silence is the light by which the mind finds its way
in the city of our ignorance, in the night of fear
and folly when apes mistake cacophony for music.

At 120 decibels the hair cells in the cochlea succumb
to any noise and you cannot hear silence any more.
Now see if your eyes can hear the last gasp of creation
about 13.75 gigayears ago when you were born to die.

Where Are the Dreams?

Where are the dreams that didn't make it across
the border between night and knowledge? Those
that give me the slip at the first sign of light and leave
only a dark sense of their absence as though a black stone
had dropped through a lake surface – are they cosmic
realities where we live another life without knowing?

What of the dreams that don't exist here at all?
Technicians wire your sleep and record the faintest tremor
under your skull to prove that you dreamt, but you scour
your mindscape in the pale light of dawn in vain
for any trace of image or happening, memory or thought.

We are walking galaxies of a hundred trillion cells: each
may contain a cosmos as rich and complex as the one
we're dreaming now. What if worm-holes open in our brain
at night so we can travel to a universe in another dimension?

All That's Possible

If the crow swooping down from an elm tree to scavenge
a cadaver here can trigger a tsunami in the Sea of Japan,
how many volcanoes will erupt because we made love?

Cannot then the bomb that levels someone's home
reverberate across event horizons to inspire a history
in which lovers meet to live in bliss forever after?

All things interact in an intricate mesh of motions
looped and bent at random into a net knotted by laws
that rule chaos out of order to catch every star in the sky.

All that's possible happens, for every quark must move
on multiple paths so that every imaginary history is real
though we perceive only the shadow of their sum total.

Somewhere there is a world in which you are Cleopatra
and I'm the snake you took to your bosom to save yourself.

Parallels

Off the west coast of Africa shysharks shrink
from danger into a tight circle till their tails
cover their eyes and they drift blind to the threat
perceived, a wheel of fish turning and turning
away from what they don't want to know:
the beast whose greed for life will devour them
fish eye to fish eye with their feigned ignorance.

Up on land, across the ocean, creatures more flesh
than fish or fowl crowd the mad merry-go-round
of money and self-gratification spinning faster and
faster till they too can see no more the devastation
or the dying which are their own doing and undoing.

Spacetime curves all parallels back unto themselves
till they meet in the infinity between here and then.

On the Head of a Pin

In a place where any finite stretch can be divided
infinitely, nothing should come as a surprise – such as
the hundred billion galaxies with a hundred billion stars
and their satellites each, dancing on the head of a pin
a nanosecond after nothing troubled the void to try
something, try becoming something, take a chance and
dance worlds into being where living is the same as dying.

Fast-forward ten billion years or so when the palpable dark
stays the flight of stars and the universe holds its breath
before the arrow of time is reversed and everything returns
to the beginning. How long will the stars hold still and stop
life dead in its tracks? An eternity? Then, when the great
contraction begins, will everything run in reverse? Shall we
be born from our graves and return screaming to the womb?

The big crunch will be a crushing bore because
when the entire cosmos ends up on the head of a pin
spacetime will implode and nothing will ever have been.

A Troubled Mirror

The alternative is that there isn't as much
of what we don't know what it is or whether
it's there as there would have to be to crunch
all cosmic numbers into zero. In that case
everything would continue to fly apart
until every star is an island unto itself
afloat in an expanding bubble of darkness.

Yesterday's glaciers left this giant rock
against which we lean and watch the moon
dance across a lake of molten snow and ice
that mimics a troubled mirror in your eyes.

Why are the stars running away from us, love?
Why did the infinite night wash us ashore here?
To learn to be more gentle with the world?

Domes of Darkness

Here you walk in the footsteps of a shadow you can't shake;
it follows or precedes you everywhere, and at high noon
for a brief moment the two of you are united and inseparable.

We're rooted in darkness, and just over the edge of our senses
dome on dome of darkness, their differences in texture
and distance defined by horizons of perception, vault one
above the other in dark shells which shelter and confine us.

The darkness we can touch hovers on the other side of the first
circle – an intimate hemisphere circumscribed by the body's
three-dimensional horizons, which the fingertips know best.

The architect of the outermost cupola is the eye. Bold and impetuous,
it can take in a whole city from the top of a skyscraper or a mountain,
encompass an entire geography of rivers and their valleys, forests,
lakes, plains, even the sea, and at night it can embrace a billion stars
and galaxies all the way back to the time and place of their birth.

Between sight and touch the blind beast encounters many shades,
but beyond the eye's horizon the dark is as black as death. The mind,
guided by the radar of its inner ear, can fly there and enter

vast inner spaces lit by the suns of other worlds where you
and your shadow are forever one as they listen and dance
to the clever tunes music and mathematics play all night long.

What Is Extraordinary

1

What is extraordinary is not what is extraordinary –
not flying machines which shatter the glass barriers
of eternal silence in the heavens, not the steel and stone
towers which cannot scrape even the surface of the sky,
not mighty empires built by men sick with elephantiasis
of *amour-propre*, not the mega-projects pursued in boardrooms
by the mickey-mouse minds of mega-egos, not the fake realities
fabricated in film studios to sedate minds apt to wonder
why what they see is not what they get – all this
is sideshow and circus to distract and entertain you to death.

The melodies of Mozart like the flowering of marigold
and the tumescence of your member are manufactured
by purple bacteria supplying cellular energy to transcribe
a three-letter code chosen from GUCA – the alphabet of life.

2

What is extraordinary is what is ordinary: the hand
which does not know or care why or how it moves
across this page; a loaf of bread, freshly baked, smelling
of summer fields sun and rain teased into grain; the wind
surfing the green waves of forests; a slender flute turning
someone's breath into music; a smile on your face; the feel
of polished wood; the memory of a loved one long departed;
or just plain walking barefoot by the beach or across a meadow
unable to read the Braille of grass and sand – these are the horizons
of innocent experience which harbour all our fugitive lives.

Beyond them, darkness prevails where universes expand
and contract forever and we shall never know nor even
be able to recall how extraordinary our swift flight was
across the confined living-space of this uncanny universe.

II

FUGITIVE

... guiding the night in for a slow, soft landing ...

If I Had Known

If I had known or dreamt before that I was born
to become human meant to think and thinking
meant to learn to know that you cannot comprehend
what is what and where and why and who you are

would I've torn myself from the sheltering dark
to step into this loud and blinding light and see
only what isn't there, hear only what happens
between a whisper and a bang and a long sleep?

The histories the mind writes are based on misleading
information and offer false clues, yet the tales they tell
supply roses with fragrance, oceans with melancholy
and the silence of empty spaces with song and laughter.

Lovers know to plant an acorn in the bush garden
as they dream of begetting another dance on the night.

A Passing Fancy

The universe is a passing fancy, whether you and I
sit by its banks and muddy the waters with our desires
or we climb the mind's peaks and stare at our horizons
of ignorance, there's no telling reality from dream.

Every second the sun burns a hundred million tons
of hydrogen into helium; another couple of months
into the cosmic calendar the entire solar system will be
a thin veil of fire spreading, scattering at 50 km/sec
till all is lost in the vast, icy darkness of interstellar space.

Chromosome 14 manufactures telomeres – meaningless
terminal stretches of gene which repeat TTAGGG
a few thousand times over, and as perpetual splicing
cuts them short and shorter, they determine how
and when we age. The fountain of youth is gibberish.

Ghost Particles

As I write and you read this, billions of neutrinos pass
through us, hurled by the sun across space with such force
and so little energy they can pass through a trillion miles
of lead without their path being slowed or deflected –
ghost particles, they come and go without leaving a trace.

You and I are ghost particles of and in another dimension.
The bacteria that move the blood where it is needed and
transcribe waves and particles into a sensible whole
are as incomprehensible to us as we are to them.

Here we are, surrounded by our failure to understand what
the silence of galaxies and our own self-destruction teach:
not intelligence but love confers an evolutionary advantage.
Holding hands we are a bridge from one side to the other
of equations the cosmos cannot solve by its own axioms.

Put Things into Words

In his confessions he admitted that he knew things
were what they were so long as no one asked him.
The simplest question would plunge him into darkness.
What is time? Who are you? Time is a river, mist
rising, rain falling, and you forever in and of the flow.
From where to where is not the question, it's the answer.

If you can put things into words, what does that say
about the nature of things? Words are envelopes,
sound enough to stuff with detailed labels and directions,
but too slim to accommodate the things themselves.

Where does that leave us and them? In the river which knows
its rapids and its eddies because it doesn't know it flows
and turns the wheel of fortune which raises us from darkness
to the blinding light and returns things there in time.

My Heart This Solo

Where did my heart pick up that low measured beat?
It drums me through a jungle of so many lives,
all different, all possible, then calls me uniquely
to be me when I want to be them, all of them.

Like some blind beast stalking an elusive light
my heart drums through a jumble of what seems possible:
a slow, relentless march from some place out of mind
here where fields and forests are the measure of all things.

That soft, thudding footfall began as the quick-step
of some wild, frightened thing running from the night
when I was cast breathless upon a lonely shore.

It was before that, long before the trauma of earth
and air that the heartless sea taught me to dance,
taught my heart this solo to a darkly slowing beat.

It's All So Simple

It's all so simple. The instructions are there
in a zillion sets of do-it-yourself books,
and all things alive follow them to a T –
replication, translation, auto-correction,
all recorded in very simple language using
just four letters to form three-letter words.

The alphabet of being – you don't need brains
to read it. Every plant, every animal does it
without giving it a thought.
                                On second thought,
the more of it you read the better your chances
of getting a brain. It's all so simple if it weren't
so complex. That's why so far we've mastered

only the language of death. It's even simpler.
Its alphabet consists of a single letter: capital *I*.

Chains of Amino Acids

Don't underestimate the scheming power of genes:
they're as ruthlessly conniving as they are microscopic.
The medal you want to give the man for his macho deed
should be awarded to the twisted piece of DNA
that codes for courage, chains of amino acids, exons,
RNA, polypeptides, proteins. Your hero is pathetic,
helpless to disobey the orders of his egomaniacal genes
that drive him to thread his seed through a zillion ovaries
into the future. How else to understand the death-defying
fortitude of a woman bearing, nursing, rearing her young.

Hand in hand they walk into a future that has no future,
led up the garden path of a paradise that never will be.
Their faith in the faith that's never moved a mountain
compels them to climb relentlessly up the double helix.

Family Tree

I doubt you could fit our family tree on the mainsails of a frigate because
my ancestors, on both my mother's and my father's side, I can trace
all the way back to RFW. Some gaps are still waiting to be filled in,
but genetic finger-printing and the fossil record are clear and conclusive.

RFW lived between 520 and 540 million years ago and was a roundish
flatworm crawling about mudflats in a Precambrian biotech laboratory
where they hit upon the Hox genes, an ingenious solution to a staggering
embryonic problem: what to grow next when and where from identical cells.

You can thank your lucky Hox genes your eyes are not on your heels for they
determine the two asymmetries of your body: front to back, and mouth to
anus. They're lined up so that each homeotic gene switches on the next one
in the order in which the embryo grows. Without the Hox genes life might've

turned out to be a hoax. It's so brilliantly simple and open-ended that all RFW's
descendants inherited clusters of the same Hox genes – frogs, flies, dinosaurs,
   rats,
us. All nature had to do was add a cluster or two to make the difference. RFW
probably had only one Hox set, flies have eight, we thirteen. We're all glorified

worms. What distinguishes us from them was added at the rear-end. So it's
entirely fitting that we end up closing the circle by providing a meal for them.

Interlocus Contest Evolution

Not love, but life conquers all – all that can be
taken by storm or stealth and permits domicile.
Love is a strategy of the genes to send a message
to the end of time: they are the message.

My mother signed the treaty with an X,
my father with a Y. I am the short-lived truce
in an aeons-old war between gender-mad genes
that plot and scheme to checkmate each other.

Put your mouth to my sex and speak to me of love.
I will roam the hills and valleys of your flesh
in a delirium that will transport us beyond contest
to an alternative cosmos where time stands still.

I hear bells toll. My chromosomes are calling: they that
masculate my brain muscle my body for love and war.

Convexed and Concaved

Whom the sun does not blind can see but he cannot
ever walk through the glass dividers of the five senses.
Listen to the night music stars make in the spheres
and touch the tip of your nose slowly with your toe

or try to smell your way out of a mirror. You'll not
find this labyrinth to your taste where at every step
you encounter yourself convexed and concaved
grimacing at your self with a monkey on your back.

Why does the mind mislead us into thinking the un-
thinkable? Your eyes won't show you the way out
unless you bury your face in the hills of her breasts.

Only the self that learns to fly updrafts of love
can soar above the peaks of thought and look back
with tears in his eyes and laughter ringing in her ears.

Between Nowhere and Now

Now, so many decades later, what matters most
has settled into spaces I can visit only in my wildest
dreams – memories with the fragrance of a kiss
whose lips linger between nowhere and now.

Where are the things which are neither here nor there?
A fragment from a string quartet abuts a street
scene through a window and in the space between
the silk swish of a dress slides forever to the floor.

That music and this embrace are eternal for they are
always now and never. Yesterday is a film time edits
mercilessly, leaving for tomorrow's screen nothing

but phantoms in a moonlit night. Memory makes us
who we have always been: a play of mask and mime
performed in an implausible space in the nick of time.

Memory Plays Tricks

Don't forget that memory plays tricks on us.
A motion picture is a sequence of stills.
A horse racing is motionless at every point
you take its picture, and since the space between
two points can be divided infinitely the horse
stands still at all times. Memory creates motion.

Or else time and space are more than the sum
of their infinite points – an indivisible whole.
In which case you cannot be here, or there,
or anywhere, now or ever. Where are you then,
love, if there is no place for you in this world
of conundrums which cannot do without us?

Memory draws the line that defines the horizon
where you first appeared, and holds us together.

Alarming Possibilities

This frigid dawn stares at me with the dark protruding
eyes of deer. Not a glint in them of the dagger winter
has drawn, pointing its ice-edged tip at all living hearts.
The deer scrape snow with graceful hoof from buried grass.

Cut to an extreme close-up of the heart of the matter,
the grey matter, that composes the cosmos firing synapses.
Then a fast tracking shot of an idea launched on an impulse.
Count down to zero and we have lift-off to another hypothesis.

I know you think I think too much. Would you rather listen
to the stickmen lie about the games they play with power?
I go for a poem any time; it talks without ulterior motives.

The universe is full of alarming possibilities in the eyes of deer.
To my mind it's a mathematical equation that proves nothing
and can predict nothing. The deer flee in the grey fur of twilight.

Maybe, Maybe Not

Don't you believe it – the future is no more predictable
than the roll of a die. A butterfly winging it in Borneo
may per chance blow the roof off your bungalow
on the banks of the Ottawa river, or it may not.
Such is the calculated charm of infinite numbers

in a finite world. You and I are part of the equation
that cannot accurately predict the weather or prove
our existence. Maybe, maybe not. We're half
responsible for everything. Nothing can be proved
right except the darkness at the end of the tunnel.

Let a snowflake melt on your tongue and taste
the cosmos. Tell me what kind of a kiss that is.

It takes all our energy to stay alive. Embracing
each other maybe we can keep warm. Or maybe not.

The Final Word

To know that you cannot know what you know
is a problem only if you forget your ignorance.

We inhabit a mind that is a mansion built on a hill
in no-man's-land, with many rooms whose doors
are locked and windows shuttered, waiting for you
to dare the unthinkable and venture outside.

To discover yourself is to pull the cover off the bed
on which you lie and find what you see is what you love.

What you hear is as questionable as what you say.
You were born with grammar on your brain, but
you picked the words from Pandora's box of illusions.

The final word is that there is no final word.
There you are, here I am, and if we love each other
we may eventually learn to ask the right questions.

No One Has Ever

No one has ever seen or heard a quark. They hide deep inside
the atom they create and maintain. Maybe on the morning
of November 1, 1952, on the Pacific atoll of Eniwetok
they were exposed, but no living thing survived the blast to tell.

My hand cupping your breast cannot feel any quark,
nor can I detect the taste of any deep inside your mouth.
Yet mathematics and our faith in reason demand their existence.
They are, after all, the building blocks of the entire universe.

I can't blame you if you don't believe a word I'm saying.
You seem to understand the trouble with words, how they claim
and pretend to be true only to point you in the wrong direction.

Is it possible that the universe is an infinite recession of worlds
within worlds, in each of which a pair of lovers is stretched out
against the sky like a pair of lovers stretched out against the sky?

The Meaning of Irrelevancy

Don't despair because you discover your meaningless life.
What did you expect? Angels to attend your birth? None will
trumpet your death either. Believe me, God is thinkable only
to minds cringing before the glorious terror of the universe.

Its vast machinations make us irrelevant for they feed into
infinity and on that scale we cannot be perceived. Nor is it
relevant that the man in the moon cannot register our existence.
The meaning of irrelevancy is the irrelevancy of meaning.

Open the window and let in dawn. Birds are singing if you say so.
If you say so, clouds will wrestle the wind high up in the sky
and by the pond wild geese mate for life. Because you say
so the river is running rapids to pour out its heart to the sea.

Don't despair because you have invented the universe.
Imagine an energy field where you couldn't tell a rose.

The Letter "e"

Someone told him that words are merely signposts pointing
to what cannot be said. Even what they name – encounters,
events, ideas, the objects themselves, it was said, are no more
than innuendos of what might be something or somewhere else.

The alphabet of the universe starts with the letter "e" for energy
and existence. $E = mc^2$ is the explanation. You need the speed of light
to establish anything: ego, eros, element, error, entropy, evil, etcetera.

He was on a quest for the truth and wanted to learn the language
in which the stars talk to trees and rivers. So he listened, recorded
what he heard, and digitalized everything to pack it into a chip
which he swallowed so he might become knowledge pure and simple.

Instead, he found himself a digit among digits. And nothing changed,
the proportions, the words stayed the same. Except he was now
without emotion. He no longer knew he was part of the puzzle.

He Discovered Darkness

He discovered darkness could be a terrifying monster the day
his mother locked him in the cellar for some childish offense.
In the beginning there was the experience of perfect peace

of which he recalled only the absence of absolutely everything,
including himself. Which made perfect sense. There was no fear
and no hope because there were no questions. This darkness lasted
forever and he might never have known he had ever been there.

But then the dark moved, twitched and twisted, and he awoke to a soft
rhythmic drumming, like someone calling him over and over, the same
voice troubling and comforting him. He was floating in a cocoon of black
feathers which were caressing and choking him at the same time.

Then something happened. A sharp instrument severed him from eternity,
night shattered, and shards of light revealed a darkness alive with demons.
He found himself screaming without knowing why or how he got there.

Success Story

He knows what it's like to know all the answers
because his questions spring from them like amaryllis
from their bulbs. But he no longer knows that he knows
for he no longer roots in the ground. Like a honey-bee
he's energized by flowers and his quest leaves trails
as invisible as a buzz to the hive where he must store
what he needs for the coming winter of the mind.

In spring his hands were intimate with stone, carved it
in the shapes of his spirit, and tethered the sacred bull
in earth colours to the walls and ceilings of dark caves.

His hands knew the answer before any questions arose,
so his summer was a success story. Till his grasp exceeded
his reach and he separated knowing from his knowledge.

There was nothing left to harvest in the fall but solitude.

Imperfect Recall

In his dreams he found faces
were often out of focus;
he needed glasses to recognize them.

When his ophthalmologist asked him
to recall his mother, long dead
and buried, it was discovered

he required a prescription,
but only for his right eye.
The imperfections he saw
were in the lens, not in the past.

In his left eye the imagination
proved to have 20/20 vision still.

Now he wears a monocle to bed,
looking for himself as a child.

A Long Shot

He was tired of running after meanings.
All his long life he'd aimed words carefully
but always they'd fallen short of the target.

Thinking, he decided, was too rigid a bow
to send his words flying with enough force
to find the bull's eye. Or was his aim poor?

What if the centre of things was a black hole
deeper than thought, which swallowed words
and gave back nothing? So he fell silent

and listened. Slowly his ears brought the world
into focus and something he heard told him
the archer was also the arrow and the target.

He pulled back for a long shot of his childhood and found himself
under an apple tree, both fruit and the ground on which it dropped.

Revolution & Evolution

Those who believe revolution is the road to redemption
are just as right as those who put their faith in evolution
– and just as wrong. It takes both to move mountains
or to metamorphose amoebae into Eve and Adam.

But there is no redemption in the Elysian spaces of time.
For three billion years the elements were mixed and remixed,
whipped, boiled, and distilled in the laboratories
of primeval oceans till by an alchemist's stroke of luck

something blew up in the face of our stony planet and scattered
hosts of bizarre creatures everywhere: the Precambrian
miracle put life on the road to us. The rest is history,

discontinuous and elusive as memory and not flattering
to you, Venus and Adonis, for the road leads past you
and beyond you. Another revolution is evolving inexorably.

Stranded in Disneyland

Hold on to your heads, fellow-travellers!
The winds of change have whipped up a tornado
that's touched down in our mind's settlements,
picking up everything we know and forcing it
through a furious funnel whose centre holds
only long enough to spin all into fragments
and scatter them across the entire galaxy.

Who d'you think is going to pick up the pieces
and put Humpty-Dumpty back together again?

The times are out of joint. What will happen
yesterday took place tomorrow. Today is
a fashion the mind creates for want of options.

We've come to the wrong place. We were looking
for paradise and ended up stranded in Disneyland.

Time Loops

The moment I put pen to paper is gone
the moment I put pen to paper.
Every hour disappears in the crack
between before and after, invisible
to the naked eye. Like Schrödinger's cat
time is not there when it is there when it's not.

Where does that leave you and me peering
through a crack in an ancient Chinese vase
at the Ming dynasty? A crack too thin
to leak water but wide enough for an army
of terracotta warriors. How can we know
if our love will last till death do us part?

There is one chance in an exponential trillion
zeros we can loop back to before we were born.

Refugee

Alongside the road runs a ditch that is chockfull
of abandoned dreams, worn-out hopes, broken
promises, and tattered illusions. Here and there
he finds something which he can't fix, or a spare part
which is still usable, but he doesn't know where it goes
and the mule pulling his cart refuses to let him pile more
junk on a load already taxing its strength to the limit.

Eventually, the stubborn beast stops and lies down
in the middle of the road. There is nothing now for him
to do but sit on a milestone and watch the slow stream
of refugees fleeing the ignorant tyranny in their villages
for the freedom of a truth they'll never reach. He dozes

off and dreams another dimension where he discovers
he would've done better to stay home with what he loved.

A Dream Vision

He dreamt he was an eagle and someone was calling him:
Wake up, the voice said, *open your eyes, see for yourself!*
When he did that, what he saw terrified him, and he clung
to the notion that opening your eyes does not end a dream:

he was caught in a trap, he had lost his wings, and his body
was without feathers; the trap was a square box with walls
hard as stone but not of stone; it was filled with loud noise,
and there was an opening, blocked by a strange creature
rearing on its hindlegs; its skin was composed of patches
of short hair, curly, bushy, in odd places, top and bottom;
its beak was broken off and from the wound in its face

the voice uttered: *I'll be you and you'll be me, give or take
a few mutations.* Then it moved aside, and he escaped back
to his eyrie in the luminous silence between mountain peaks,
keeping the eyes of his dream shut so he could look for prey.

Sisyphus

(to Stefan Fichert for his drawings)

It's not the herculean labour of rolling a huge stone up a steep slope
every day that he experiences as pain and punishment, nor is it
the frustration of knowing it'll roll back down again the instant
he lets go – it's his inability to discover and comprehend why.

As a son of the wind he was bound to tell the river-god his daughter
was raped by Zeus. Or was it because later he fathered Odysseus?

He thinks of himself as a child of the stars, and if he had not been
inquisitive, prolific and restless, he couldn't have travelled from there
to this green valley he now calls home. To get here he negotiated
countless disasters which might've ended his journey long before his time.

He has carved the word *WHY* into the boulder and watches the light
striate its grooves and planes as he struggles to push it uphill. He tastes
the sweat on his lips, listens to the wind, and smiles: it no longer matters
that the ancient myth-makers are dead and their stories inscrutable now.

He rejoices in knowing his senses make sense of what makes no sense.

Homo patheticus

Whatever happened to *Homo sapiens,* that brainy creature who moved
two-legged out of Africa to occupy every niche on the planet?
Something cataclysmic must've happened for them to disappear
all of a sudden around ten thousand years ago and mutate.
What exactly was the nature of the neolithic catastrophe? A meteor shower
of radioactive material causing a mass mutation in this one species?

After the event a new species emerged – *Homo patheticus,* mindless
animals suffering severe delusional disorders: they think they own everything –
    rivers, plains, forests, even the mountains along with the sky their peaks
    puncture; they devour every fruit, every plant, every animal that feeds their
    pride;
they carve up continents, oceans, even the heavens, and claim sovereignty
by flying flags; they train hordes of slaves to defend what a ruling elite owns,
equips them with weapons and in moronic ecstasy orders them to conquer
more cities, more kingdoms, more land, more water, more air,
and to kill as many of their own unkind kind as they possibly can.
As a final triumphant gesture they poison the food they eat, the water
they drink, and the air they breathe to devastate their own habitat.

There is evidence to suggest that at the threshold to the neolithic
the world crossed into a reverse energy field which converted everything
from positive to negative: earth into anti-earth peopled by anti-humans
ruled by anti-reason. *Homo sapiens* moved to imaginary spacetime
on the other side of a black hole where they plan to settle the void.

Life in Virtual Space

When the inhabitants of the antiworld saw what was happening
they prepared to migrate to the planet their counterparts had abandoned
for life in virtual space. No one could tell which was the shadow
of the other and it made no difference because by then wind and rain
had scratched beyond recognition the faces of the steel and stone
structures they left behind and things plastic were bleached in tatters.

The toxic air and water proved to be manna for *antihomo antisapiens*
and soon they occupied every niche in the new bleak and wasted world.

Meanwhile the original inhabitants had made themselves at home
in virtual reality where they were visible only to themselves.
There they achieved absolute freedom from the vagaries of the old order
that had consigned them to the banalities of breeding and dying.

But in virtual space they could only virtually come into existence.
The new race in the old world never knew they were not real.

Midnight

The hour strikes twelve. An icy wind is scratching
the night's scalp with sharp claws. Silently, the stars drift
to the earth's shoulders where night's black hand
brushes them off like dandruff. It's winter up north.

You turn your dreams over cold in your sleep, hand them
to the care of a crescent moon which cuts the most memorable
scenes from the life you live in a world with fugitive horizons
where you find the best and the worst
are always about to come to pass and never do.

Draw the covers over your head when you shiver.
You don't want to be confined to a clock.
You don't need to listen to the haunting footsteps
that stalk you. They echo dream worlds without end.

Nightmare Tomorrow

It's already yesterday when it should've been
the day after tomorrow. Time has come and gone
around the bend ever since we will have added
that new dimension to what is and will be real.

I'm full of passion for you so many years after
we will have been married that I no longer know
whether I'll be in love with you then and/or now
until I can slip the past back into the future.

The apple trees are forever blossoming in winter
and frogs are mute and mutant in the summer nights.
November mists drift swiftly into April showers
because the sun is wearing fall colours the year round.

Why is it that in my dreams tonight everything unreal
is real while the real world is tomorrow's nightmare?

Hallucinate Oblivion

(for John by way of an answer)

And now your fireflies arrive and swarm all over
this warm summer evening waving strobe-lights
as if to take the measure of me and this maple grove
before guiding the night in for a slow soft landing –
a vast black unidentified flying object from outer space
looming, silent, its myriad windows ablaze with starlight.

If only I could read the flash code of their tiny fires,
perhaps I could learn how to ask the right questions,
those the stars urge on us. What happened the minute before
a supercharged event flung a billion galaxies into the void?
Could all that energy instead have imploded and vanished
into a negative dimension? Why are we here and not there?

Perhaps the night is the answer. I shall plant cereus cacti
and intoxicated by their singular bloom hallucinate oblivion.

Renaissance

When finally the lights went out in their cities, the stars
returned to sing in the deserted streets. An east wind blew up
and accompanied them hoarsely like a shakuhachi flute to restore
the long lost silence in which the stones' voices can be heard.

Scarred and disfigured, the forests too recovered; a host
of worms, ants, and beetles facilitated the return of fallen trees
to earth. Burns healed as green leaves repossessed the light
and remodelled it in a canopy for the reawakening world.

At dawn the birds reassessed and celebrated survival chances
and in the greening air spiders hummed in their webs, watching
ferns unfurl and fan the savoury smell of moss. Dew regained
its taste of pure spring, and everywhere deer and foxes felt reborn.

Of the beast whose insatiate appetite had almost devoured all,
few remained, speechless, relearning the language of the wilderness.

Woodcut

The woodcut by my desk stares down at me
with a stern face in profile, the eye as deep
and unfathomable as the black hole in the centre
of our galaxy: the artist looking at his image
trembling on a mirror's membrane that divides
what he wants to know from what he knows.

Dark the energy that propels his hand, dark
the matter that obsesses his heart. He carves
in wood the five percent of the world he can see
feel smell taste hear – the rest is darkness,
dark matter, dark energy stalking his mind
in the white void between the lines in his face.

Like summer wind bending wheatfields into golden waves,
the overwhelming darkness dances universes into dreams.

Fugitive Horizons

We're hemmed in on all sides by horizons.
Whichever way we turn – east, west, north or south
– a fine line separates us from the stars.

Sometimes a horizon hides behind a city,
a range of mountains or a stand of trees.
You try to sneak up on it and go to the top
of the tallest building or you climb the highest
peak to take it by surprise – there it is, farther
away than ever, the edge of the known world.

Timespace is yet another horizon as fugitive
as every dimension mind can conceive.

Horizons surround us like a mobile fence and keep their distance.
Try to approach one and it will flee as fast as you can run,
faster than your thoughts can fly. Catch a horizon and die.

Why Should There Be More

Why should there be more or less than meets the eye
here on this god-forsaken rock spinning uncontrollably
at the outer limits of a galaxy remarkable only for being
unremarkable? Here what is there is what it is, and more.
We enter this world through the portals of perception

and we cannot forsake our senses, pilots across turbulent
oceans of uncertain particles. Theirs is the power
to turn drab energies into the glory of countless worlds
the mind translates into ecstasies and agonies:

the convoluted ear composes vibrations into symphonies,
the subtle eye creates art's and nature's visions of beauty
from insubstantial photons, and the keen nose finds pheromones
in a skunk's defences to spray Arabia's intoxicating perfumes,
while the nimble tongue names all it can and cannot taste.

Where else in the universe could hands too gross to pluck
Planck-length strings into music learn to love? Not, surely,
in the towers of high speculation and mighty hypotheses,
behind whose walls and gates senses make no sense, and
only mathematics makes sense of the stories the senses tell.

There may be a path of truth out of the labyrinth of numbers
and calculations, but I'd as soon listen to the wind humming
dawn's tune in a pine or the rain's dance and patter on the roof.

Night Song

Tonight the moon is but a thin chalk mark in the sky –
an apostrophe followed by an 's' for silence, stillness, sleep.

Take your lover by the hand and go down to the dock, forget the universe,
let the glittering stars blindfold you, let the night's frosty silence
plug your ears, for out there in the invisible spaces of the visible cosmos
a hundred supernovae explode every second, each with enough force
to burst every eardrum within a billion miles and incinerate as many planets.

Enjoy the tranquillity darkness delivers on the lake's smooth surface,
for beneath it atoms move at a frenzied pace, colliding with each other
more than a hundred billion times a second. The perpetual tornadoes
at the heart of matter would spin you out of mind. There are more atoms
in a teaspoon of water than there are drops of water in all the world's oceans.

Believe me, you do well not to want to be cured. To be blind and deaf
to within inches of the little world we inhabit is a blessing.
An instant over the horizon of our perceptions would annihilate us.

Believe what you see. Stare, stare in the black mirror of the lake.
The moon lies on it light and hushed as a loon's feather, with not a breath
to ruffle it. Nothing stirs, not even the fish in the dark deep. Only
our ghosts, imperturbable, wide-eyed, stare back at us, wondering.

Acknowledgements

My deepest thanks go, as always, to my wife Arlette Francière. Despite her own commitments to work as a painter and as a translator, she has enthusiastically shared the dizzying pursuit of so many fugitive horizons. Without her I might well have lost my way among them.

About the Author

Henry Beissel is a poet, playwright, essayist, translator and editor whose writing first came to national attention through the controversial political/literary journal *Edge* which he founded in Edmonton, Alberta, and edited from 1963 to 1969. Since then he has over thirty publications to his credit, including twenty volumes of poetry; six books of plays, both for adults and young audiences; translations from the works of Bauer, Huchel, Ibsen, Mrozek, and Dorst; fiction and non-fiction; a book on Canada; a Festschrift for Irving Layton; and two anthologies of plays for high schools. His work has been translated into more than a dozen languages. His first book of poetry was *New Wings for Icarus,* the very first book published by Coach House Press in 1966. His most recent collection is *Seasons of Blood,* published in 2011 by Buschekbooks.

Beissel has been awarded many prizes, including, in November 1994, the first Walter-Bauer Literaturpreis in Germany for his translations of Bauer's poetry and for his own literary *oeuvre*. In October 2006, he received First Prize in Poetry for "The Jade Canoe" in an international competition adjudicated by the Surrey International Writers' Conference. In 2008, he was awarded the Naji Naaman Literary Prize for his book-length poem, "Where Shall the Birds fly?" and became an honorary member of the *Maison Naaman pour la Culture* in Beirut, Lebanon.

Praise for Henry Beissel's Writing

"Henry Beissel is undoubtedly a Canadian poet of the first rank. He writes with the clarity and precision demanded of a strict imagist, and yet manages, without over-burdening the issue, to give the image symbolic weight." – Patrick White

"The Canadian imagination, as elusive as the Canadian identity, is nevertheless a reality. Henry Beissel finds its constant source of strength and renewal in the wonder of our northland ... This epic is the first to see it in its entirety, as a matrix which binds the whole together in a national mythology." – F.R. Scott (on *Cantos North*)

"*Season of Blood* is one of the most powerful, moving, lyrical triumphs in modern poetry." – Keith Garebian

Printed in August 2013
by Gauvin Press,
Gatineau, Québec